QuoteOctopus.com

Published by Matthew North

When you focus on being a blessing, God makes sure that you are always blessed in abundance.

Joel Osteen

Whatever we are waiting for - peace of mind, contentment, grace, the inner awareness of simple abundance - it will surely come to us, but only when we are ready to receive it with an open and grateful heart.

Sarah Ban Breathnach

The test of our progress is not whether we add more to the abundance of those who have much it is whether we provide enough for those who have little.

Franklin D. Roosevelt

Doing what you love is the cornerstone of having abundance in your life.

Wayne Dyer

I try to be grateful for the abundance of the blessings that I have, for the journey that I'm on and to relish each day as a gift.

James McGreevey

We are buried beneath the weight of information, which is being confused with knowledge; quantity is being confused with abundance and wealth with happiness.

Tom Waits

Abundance is not something we acquire. It is something we tune into.

Wayne Dyer

Abundance is a process of letting go; that which is empty can receive.

Bryant H. McGill

Talent is always conscious of its own abundance, and does not object to sharing.

Aleksandr Solzhenitsyn

Your most precious, valued possessions and your greatest powers are invisible and intangible. No one can take them. You, and you alone, can give them. You will receive abundance for your giving.

W. Clement Stone

The abundance of cheap food with low nutritional value in the Western diet has wreaked havoc on our health; in America, one third of children and two thirds of adults are overweight or obese and are more likely to develop diabetes and cardiovascular disease.

Ellen Gustafson

What is called genius is the abundance of life and health.

Henry David Thoreau

If God has given you the world's goods in abundance, it is to help you gain those of Heaven and to be a good example of sound teaching to your sons, servants, and relatives.

Saint Ignatius

What we need to do is really improve energy efficiency standards, develop in full scale renewable and alternative energy and use the one resource we have in abundance, our creativity.

Lois Capps

Life in abundance comes only through great love.

Elbert Hubbard

The world is full of abundance and opportunity, but far too many people come to the fountain of life with a sieve instead of a tank car... a teaspoon instead of a steam shovel. They expect little and as a result they get little.

Ben Sweetland

You pray in your distress and in your need; would that you might also pray in the fullness of your joy and in your days of abundance.

Khalil Gibran

When I think about creating abundance, it's not about creating a life of luxury for everybody on this planet; it's about creating a life of possibility. It is about taking that which was scarce and making it abundant.

Peter Diamandis

Today we have access to highly advanced technologies. But our social and economic system has not kept up with our technological capabilities that could easily create a world of abundance, free of servitude and debt.

Jacque Fresco

Many a man curses the rain that falls upon his head, and knows not that it brings abundance to drive away the hunger.

Saint Basil

The key to abundance is meeting limited circumstances with unlimited thoughts.

Marianne Williamson

We live in a world of constant juxtaposition between joy that's possible and pain that's all too common. We hope for love and success and abundance, but we never quite forget that there is always lurking the possibility of disaster.

Marianne Williamson

Great abundance of riches cannot be gathered and kept by any man without sin.

Desiderius Erasmus

I noted that people are happy here in India. When I went back home, people had everything in the materialistic sense and were surrounded with abundance, but they were not happy.

Goldie Hawn

There is an abundance of misinformation, exaggeration, and blatant lies being spread by interest groups regarding the prospects for embryonic stem cell research.

Virginia Foxx

Like the skyscraper, the automobile, and the motion-picture palace, neon signs once symbolized popular hopes for a new era of technological achievement and commercial abundance. From the 1920s to the 1950s, neon-lit streets pulsed with visual excitement from Vancouver to Miami.

Virginia Postrel

The harvest of old age is the recollection and abundance of blessing previously secured.

Marcus Tullius Cicero

Instead, I have an abundance mentality: When people are genuinely happy at the successes of others, the pie gets larger.

Stephen Covey

Expect your every need to be met. Expect the answer to every problem, expect abundance on every level.

Eileen Caddy

Advertising is an environmental striptease for a world of abundance.

Marshall McLuhan

I have never before, in my long and eclectic career, been gifted with such an abundance of natural beauty as I experienced filming 'War Horse' on Dartmoor.

Steven Spielberg

Being afraid to tell the truth because of the projected consequences, whatever it may be, shows a lack of faith and an abundance of fear.

Monica Johnson

Thank God my parents had an abundance of patience.

Lexa Doig

I don't believe in evil, I believe only in horror. In nature there is no evil, only an abundance of horror: the plagues and the blights and the ants and the maggots.

Isak Dinesen

The older generation had greater respect for land than science. But we live in an age when science, more than soil, has become the provider of growth and abundance. Living just on the land creates loneliness in an age of globality.

Shimon Peres

The decision to use a pen name was nothing more than a desire to compartmentalise my life. However, I had not thought about an appropriate pseudonym, and since there's an abundance of anagrams in the novel, the idea struck me: why not use an anagram of my name? Hence, Shawn Haigins.

Ashwin Sanghi

I live a life of gratitude for the abundance of love that I have and that 'Touched by An Angel' still has an impact that fans are still accessing.

Roma Downey

There came into the world an unlimited abundance of everything people need. But people need everything except unlimited abundance.

Karel Capek

There's an abundance of exposure when you start working in American films. Inevitably you become a brand and that has to be controlled.

Tom Hardy

From the early days of European migration to America, in the 17th Century, the prototype of buildings was based on English precedent, even if mostly translated into the locally available material in abundance: timber.

Harry Seidler

Abundance and vigor of automatic movements are desirable, and even a considerable degree of restlessness is a good sign in young children.

G. Stanley Hall

We found vines of a large size, and in some cases quite loaded with grapes; we also found an abundance of roses, which appeared to be like those of Castile.

Junipero Serra

Moreover, the abundance of chemical compounds and their importance in daily life hindered the chemist from investigating the question, in what does the individuality of the atoms of different elements consist.

Johannes Stark

Like all kids with divorced parents, I have an abundance of holidays.

Deb Caletti

Charity never lacks what is her own, all that she needs for her own security. Not alone does she have it, she abounds with it. She wants this abundance for herself that she may share it with all; and she reserves enough for herself so that she disappoints nobody. For charity is perfect only when full.

Saint Bernard

I don't need fame and I don't need power and I don't need wealth. I'm in need of friends, which I have found in abundance.

Utah Phillips

Energy is one topic on which different countries can work together collaboratively. If we can all produce energy from an element that's available in abundance on our planet, that would be a good thing, but we have to learn how to produce energy in large quantities, cheaply, efficiently and without detriment to the environment.

Mildred S. Dresselhaus

For me, the opposite of scarcity is not abundance. It's enough. I'm enough. My kids are enough.

Brene Brown

What is marriage, is marriage protection or religion, is marriage renunciation or abundance, is marriage a stepping-stone or an end. What is marriage.

Gertrude Stein

We have almost succeeded in leveling all human activities to the common denominator of securing the necessities of life and providing for their abundance.

Hannah Arendt

Sarah Palin lacked the preparation or temperament to be one heartbeat away from the presidency, but what she possessed in abundance was the ability to inflame political passions and energize the John McCain campaign with star quality.

Roger Ebert

I wish I had coined the phrase 'tyranny of choice,' but someone beat me to it. The counterintuitive truth is that have an abundance of options does not make you feel privileged and indulged; too many options make you feel like all of them are wrong, and that you are wrong if you choose any of them.

Susan Orlean

Franklin Roosevelt said the test of our progress is not whether we add more to the abundance to those who have much; it is whether we provide enough to those who have too little. This reconciliation package fails that test as well.

Patrick J. Kennedy

The Internet's abundance - of information, goods, tastes and sources of authority - creates unparalleled opportunities for individuals to get exactly what they want. But this plenitude threatens political and cultural authorities who believe in telling individuals what they can have rather than letting them choose for themselves.

Virginia Postrel

When you have too much month for you paycheck, then what you need to do is realize that there is abundance all around you and focus on the abundance and not your lack and as night follows day abundance will come to you.

Sydney Madwed

The generous abundance of her passion, without guile or trickery, was like a white flame which penetrated and found response in depths of his own sensuous nature that had never yet been reached.

Kate Chopin

Although farming of any sort was almost as impossible in the plains as in the dry regions of winter rains farther west, the abundance of buffaloes made life much easier in many respects.

Ellsworth Huntington

From the moment we were first dumped in Jamestown and had our teeth checked before getting sold off and later considered three-fifths of a human being, an abundance of 'likability' hasn't been something blacks have had to stockpile. Instead, it's been a centuries-long battle for respectability.

John Ridley

Ebooks represent a shift from a culture of scarcity to a culture of abundance. In the past, publishing required a great deal of time and energy and resources for production. Books and magazines and newspapers needed a whole industry of typesetters, editors, designers, and ultimately publishers who would decide if a book was worthy of that effort.

David Gerrold

America is a country of abundance, but our food culture is sad - based on huge portions and fast food. Let's stop with the excuses and start creating something better.

David Chang

When I left the U.S. for the first time, I spent my first year abroad in Japan. That culture shock and abundance of new stimuli combined with a lack of guidance forced me to develop my own approaches to learning and juggling.

Timothy Ferriss

I've always had an abundance of material about the subjects of my biographies.

Walter Isaacson

Wine is connected to abundance.

Carole Bouquet

When you're in danger of losing a thing it becomes precious and when it's around us, it's in tedious abundance and we take it for granted as if we're going to live forever, which we're not.

John McGahern

The best diet for overall health, and specifically for heart, brain, and cancer risk reduction, is a diet that's aggressively low in carbohydrates with an abundance of healthful fat, and this is the central theme of 'Grain Brain.'

David Perlmutter

I used to be a columnist for 'Golf Monthly' and have contributed articles for national newspapers based on the humour that is in abundance in the game, which is more than can be said of tennis.

Jasper Carrott

Free is really, you know, the gift of Silicon Valley to the world. It's an economic force, it's a technical force. It's a deflationary force, if not handled right. It is abundance, as opposed to scarcity.

Chris Anderson

The basic parts, the start-up molecules, can be supplied in abundance and don't have to be made by some elaborate process. That immediately makes things simpler.

K. Eric Drexler

When discs form around stars, there is interaction of angular momentum between disc, planets and parent star, and this interaction affects the rotation of the parent star, and that will affect the lithium abundance.

Garik Israelian

The web and physical world is plagued with abundance - people need help sorting through all the good and bad stuff out there. The tyranny of choice is causing major psychic pain and frustration for people.

Jason Calacanis

Still, I believe it is only a passing phase and cricket will one day produce an abundance of great players.

Frank Woolley

With the advent of spring and beginning of the new harvest season the creators of abundance, our peasants, come out to the fields to sow with good aspirations and hopes.

Islom Karimov

I feel that I have such an abundance in my life, and once you've seen how many people suffer and how little it takes for you to actually change their lives for the better, it's hard not to do something.

Wendie Malick

When goods are digital, they can be replicated with perfect quality at nearly zero cost, and they can be delivered almost instantaneously. Welcome to the economics of abundance.

Erik Brynjolfsson

I buy Coppertone Water Babies in abundance at the airport, SPF 60 or 70. I like being pale; I like looking like a creature from the dead world. I like looking like a ghost.

Jennifer Stone

Silicon Valley builds its bridges on abundance. Abundant bits of information floating out there, writing great programs to process it, then giving people a lot of useful tools to use it.

Robert Kyncl

The river route is certainly preferable, as it affords good grazing and an abundance of water.

William Whipple

I get an abundance of e-mail every day, some say 'dear Richard, can you call my husband, he weighs 400 pounds...' or 'my 14-year-old is 200 pounds...' or 'I just got divorced, no one wants me, I am 500 pounds.' So I pick up the phone and I call people.

Richard Simmons

I've been known to turn up drunk at triathlons and do very well. I'm more of a heat-of-the-moment type of guy. A friend will tell me about something coming up, maybe that weekend, and usually not an abundance of thought goes into my doing it.

Ryan Kwanten

The key to a vibrant middle class is an abundance of jobs that pay enough so that workers can provide for themselves and their families, enjoy leisure time, save for retirement and pay for their children's education so they can grow up and earn even more than their parents.

Marco Rubio

Thanks to the abundance of shellfish in Puget Sound, Washington State is the largest oyster producer in the country.

Tom Douglas

To eat in the same room where food is cooked - that is the way to thank the Lord for His abundance.

Paul Engle

I think there's an abundance of talent in America and there will never be not a lot of talent out there.

Randy Jackson

My parents believed in exposing each of their children to an abundance of varied activities in the hope they would find something they loved. They each had found a passion - Dad with his music and Mom with her horses - so it was natural for them to encourage experimentation.

Dorothy Hamill

For much of history it was possible to believe that the great diversity of life on Earth was a fixed creation, that the living world had never changed. But when the first stirrings of industry demanded that fuel be dug from the earth and hillsides be leveled for roads and railways, the Earth's true past was dug up in abundance.

Kenneth R. Miller

On Cape Cod, great white shark stocks have been growing, or at least becoming more concentrated, because of the multiplying numbers of seals around Monomoy Island. We are fortunate to have such abundance of these sharks in our own waters. Around the globe, we are killing in excess of 100 million sharks each year.

Brian Skerry

The first approximation in this future that we're looking at is that everyone will be physically well off. They will have a great abundance in material goods, and I think that will soften some of the conflicts we see now.

Ralph Merkle

Frankly, the only thing China has in easy abundance is people and dirty coal. Neither is the asset they're made out to be.

Thomas P.M. Barnett

We had a single find of BSE in this country. And we believe that what we're doing is appropriate action taken in an abundance of caution under the circumstances. And I believe it's the right thing to do.

Ann Veneman

Selenite occurs in abundance in well formed clear crystals of several inches in length.

George Mercer Dawson

Christmas always rustled. It rustled every time, mysteriously, with silver and gold paper, tissue paper and a rich abundance of shiny paper, decorating and hiding everything and giving a feeling of reckless extravagance.

Tove Jansson

The state of Alabama is serious about economic development, and we have shown that the Mobile region has a skilled workforce that is developing every day, strong infrastructure, and an abundance of natural resources.

Bradley Byrne